Naina's Adventure

by Enakshi Choudhuri

illustrated by Jacob Nicholas

ORBOLO BOOKS
Plymouth, Minnesota

I would like to thank my family and friends for their support and encouragement
Enakshi Choudhuri

Library of Congress Control Number: 2006931324
Choudhuri Enakshi
Naina's Adventure/ written by Enakshi Choudhuri; illustrated by Jacob Nicholas

Summary: Naina lives in America and goes on a magical journey on the Goodnight Express to visit her grandparents in India. During her adventure, she learns that as the Earth spins, day and night occur at various times in different parts of the world. Text is in two languages: English and Hindi. A pronunciation guide is provided towards the end of the book.

ISBN10: 0-9776327-0-9
ISBN13: 9780977632701

Published in the United States by
Orbolo Books
An imprint of Orbolo Educational Systems LLC
Plymouth, MN 55441 USA

www.orbolo.com

Printed and bound in India at Swapna Printing Works Pvt. Ltd., Kolkata
First Edition November 2006

Also available in English-Bengali (ISBN10: 0-9776327-1-7)
English-Gujarati (ISBN10: 0-9776327-2-5)
English-Tamil (ISBN10: 0-9776327-3-3)

For Ishani

ORBOLO
EDUCATIONAL SYSTEMS
Plymouth, Minnesota

TOOT TOOT!

Naina woke up with a start. She sat up and rubbed her eyes.

TOOT TOOT!!

There it was again! Where was that noise coming from? Naina looked around her room. Her teddy bear, Bhalu, lay on the floor just as she had left him before going to bed. She jumped up and ran to the window. The strangest sight greeted her...

In her backyard stood the most amazing train she had ever seen. Naina couldn't believe her eyes. She opened her window to take a better look.

Grey smoke rose from the apple red engine. A monkey wearing a blue and white cap grinned at her from the engine driver's window. Naina saw passenger-cars shaped like an elephant, a giraffe, a zebra, two lions side by side and even a fish! There were many people in the cars chattering excitedly with each other.

"Naina, Naina!"

"Who's calling me?" thought Naina. Suddenly she spotted her grandfather waving to her from the giraffe-shaped car.

"*Dadaji!* Grandpa! *Aap yahaan?* You're here? When did you come from India?" cried Naina.

"Shh... *Aao* Naina, *humein jaldi jaana hai,* Come, we have to leave quickly," said Dadaji.

Naina was very excited to see her grandfather. She had not seen him in more than a year. Quick as a flash she changed into her blue jeans and a T-shirt. She slipped on her shoes and ran out of the room.

TOOT TOOT!

"*Mein aa rahi hoon*! I'm coming!" exclaimed Naina softly as she flew down the stairs and out through the wide open back door to the waiting train.

" Dadaji, *Dadiji kahaan hai*? Where's Grandma?" whispered Naina, as she climbed aboard the giraffe-shaped car and hugged her grandfather.

" You'll see her very soon, Naina," said Dadaji, as he fastened her seat belt. "Now get ready for a magical ride!"

Suddenly the engine gave a long TOOOOT and the train lurched forward. Up, up it went tooting loudly.

"Dadaji, *yeh kya hai*? What's this?" asked Naina. They were high above the clouds and the sun was shining brightly now.

"Naina, this is a special train called the Goodnight Express," explained Dadaji, his eyes twinkling.

"Tell me, didn't you make a wish last night that you could visit your Dadiji and me?"

Naina stared at her grandfather, "How did you know, Dadaji?"

Dadaji smiled, "Well, Naina, your Dadiji and I were wishing we could see you too. So it looks like all our wishes are coming true."

"Dadaji, are we... no... that can't be..." Naina shook her head in disbelief.

"*Haan beta*, yes, my child. We are going to India," said Dadaji gently. "No, no, don't ask me how! It's all *jadu*, magic."

Naina thought of her last trip to India and the fun times she had shared with her grandparents and her cousins, Adi and Ria.

BEEP BEEP BEEP BEEP

Dadaji pulled out a small pager with flashing lights from his pocket.

"Dadaji, *woh kya hai?* What's that?" asked Naina, leaning forward to take a look.

"This is our beeper. Seems like our station is almost here," said Dadaji.

"*Itni jaldi?* So soon?" asked Naina doubtfully.

Suddenly the train dove through the clouds. Naina felt hundreds of butterflies in her stomach. She shouted, "Dadaji, this is just like a rollercoaster. *Mujhe bahut mazaa aa raha hai.* I'm having a lot of fun. Wheeee...!"

Naina looked down. The shapes of buildings and trees were coming closer and closer...

TOOT TOOT WHOOSH!

The Goodnight Express screeched to a halt in front of Naina's grandparents' home in India.

"Aao, beta," said Dadaji, opening the door.

"There's Dadiji," shouted Naina as she jumped down and ran towards her grandmother. "Dadiji, Dadiji, *mein aa gayee!* I'm here! Did you miss me?" she cried, holding Dadiji's hands and spinning her round and round.

"Of course, beta! Now slow down or I will fall," laughed Dadiji, hugging Naina tightly. Naina loved visiting her grandparents. But the journey from America to India was such a long one that she didn't get to see them very often. She suddenly thought of something, "Dadaji, won't Mama and Papa be worried?"

Dadaji smiled, "*Chinta muth karo*, beta. Don't worry, your parents are fast asleep and you will be home before they wake up. I'll explain later. Now, I believe your Dadiji has made a special treat for you."

The smell of hot *puris* greeted Naina as she stepped in through the front door.

"*Jaao haath dho lo,* Naina. Go wash your hands," said Dadiji, bringing bowls of hot puris and *aloo sabzi* to the table.

Naina washed her hands and sat down at the table. She scooped some puri and aloo sabzi into her mouth. "Mmmm... Dadiji, this is so yummy! Why can't you mail this to America?"

Dadiji laughed, "Now you know why you need to visit us more often, beta. *Ek aur puri logi?* Will you have another puri?"

Naina pushed her plate aside, "*Buss, aur nahin*, Dadiji. No more, I'm full."

After they had eaten, Dadaji remarked, "Naina, do you remember asking me whether Mama and Papa will worry about you coming to vist us on the Goodnight Express?"

Naina nodded.

"Well, your Dadiji and I have an experiment to show you why they will not be worried at all," said Dadaji.

Naina's eyes shone. Experiments were always a lot of fun. "Is this going to be like the sink and float experiment you showed me last year, Dadaji?"

"No, this is a different one," said Dadiji with a smile.

"Yay, *chalo,* let's go," cried Naina, as she rushed towards Dadaji's study.

"Should I close the curtains?" asked Dadiji, moving towards the window.

"*Haan, parde bandh kardo*. Yes, close the curtains," said Dadaji, as he took down an old dusty globe from his bookshelf and carefully wiped it clean. "Hmm... let me see... I think we need some light."

"There's a candle in the kitchen," murmured Dadiji. "*Mein abhi laayi.* I'll get it right away."

Dadaji placed the globe on the table. He lit the candle and placed it near the globe. "Naina, this blue globe is the Earth we all live on and this candle is the sun. Can you see how the light from the candle falls on the globe?"

Naina stared at the globe and the candle. "Yes, Dadaji, but it's only falling on one side. The other side of the globe is all dark..."

"You're right, Naina," said Dadaji. "What this means is that it is day in that part of the world where the sunlight falls and night in the part that is all dark."

Dadaji slowly spun the globe. "*Bharat kahaan hai?* Where is India? Oh, here it is... *dekho,* look Naina!" said Dadaji, pointing to India on the globe.

"*America kahaan hai,* Dadiji? Where's America?" asked Naina.

"On the other side of the globe, beta." Dadiji pointed to a spot on the darker side of the globe. "Do you see it is night in America and day in India?"

Naina nodded. Dadaji spun the globe again. "Now, tell me what you see."

"Dadaji, the light is shining on America and India has moved to the dark part," replied Naina pointing, to the globe.

"That's correct, Naina. As you observed, it is now day in America and night in India. When the Earth spins, day and night occur at various times in different parts of the world," explained Dadaji.

"Dadaji, does this mean that when we're eating breakfast in America, you're eating dinner in India?" asked Naina thoughtfully.

"Haan, beta. Do you now understand why your Mama and Papa will not be worried that you have come to visit us on the Goodnight Express?" asked Dadaji.

"Yeah, because they are fast asleep. Isn't that right, Dadaji?" asked Naina.

"*Shabash* beta, Well done. And you will be home before they wake up," said Dadaji, smiling at her.

Naina thought for a minute, "Dadaji, how come the earth doesn't get dizzy with all this spinning?"

Dadaji chuckled. "That's a good question, Naina. The earth takes one whole day and one whole night to spin around once."

"That's pretty slow, huh Dadaji? I can spin around lots of times in one minute. Dekho!" cried Naina spinning around the room.

Dadiji called from the dining room, "Who wants *gulab jamuns?*"

"Yay, gulab jamuns," shouted Naina, racing to the dining table. Her Dadiji made the best gulab jamuns in the whole world.

"Dadiji, can we go to Adi and Ria's house?" asked Naina.

"Beta, not this time... you have to go home now."

"*Kyon*, Dadiji... why? I just got here. I want to stay! Please Dadiji!" Big tears welled up in Naina's eyes.

Dadiji drew her close, "Do you remember our experiment, beta?" Naina nodded. "Well, it's going to be day in America soon. You don't want Mama and Papa to worry when they wake up, do you?"

By now Naina was beginning to feel a little sleepy. Drowsily she asked, "Dadiji, *mein ghar kaise jaaungi?* How will I go home? I don't see the Goodnight Express."

Dadaji and Dadiji began to hum a lullaby they used to sing to Naina when she was a baby. Their voices grew softer and slowly faded away, until all that remained was the faraway sound of an apple-red steam engine chugging slowly across the sky.

"Naina, *utho* beta. Get up, it's morning. School *jaana hai.* You have to go to school."

"*Abhi nahin,* Dadiji. Not now," murmured Naina sleepily.

"Beta, were you dreaming of Dadiji?" asked her mother softly.

Naina opened her eyes wide. The morning sun was streaming through the open window and her mother was sitting at the foot of her bed, smiling at her. Naina sat up in bed and rubbed her eyes in surprise. Had it all been just a dream?

What do you think?

Hindi Glossary and Pronunciation Guide

Dadaji: (daa-dah-jee) Paternal grandfather

Dadiji: (daa-dee-jee) Paternal grandmother

Mama: (maa-ma) Mother

Papa: (paa-pa) Father

Aap yahaan? (aa-p yea-haan) You are here?

Aao: (aa-oh) Come

Humein jaldi jaana hai: (hum-aein jul-dee jaa-nah hai) We have to go quickly

Mein aa rahi hoon: (maye aa rahee hoon) I am coming

Kahaan hai? (ka-haan hai) Where is?

Yeh kya hai? (yayh kya hai) What is this?

Haan: (haan) Yes

Beta: (bay-ta) My child, can be used for both boys and girls

Jadu: (jaa-doo) Magic

Woh kya hai? (woh kya hai) What is that?

Itni jaldi? (ith-nee jul-dee) So soon?

Mujhe bahut mazaa aa raha hai: (moo-jhe bahoot muh-zaa aa rahaa hai) I am having a lot of fun

Mein aa gayee: (maye aa guh-yee) I'm here or I have come

Chinta muth karo: (chin-tah muth kur-oh) Don't worry

Puris: (poo-ree) Deep fried Indian bread

Jaao haath dho lo: (jaa-oh haa-th dhough lo) Go, wash your hands

Aloo sabzi: (aa-loo sub-zee) Potato curry

Ek aur puri logi? (aek or poo-ree low-gee) Will you have another puri?

Buss, aur nahin: (bus or na-heen) Enough, no more

Chalo: (chu-loh) Let's go

Haan, parde bandh kardo: (haan, pur-dey bundh kur-though) Yes, close the curtains

Mein abhi laayi: (mai uh-bhee laa-ee) I'll get it right away.

Bharat kahaan hai? (bha-ruth ka-haan hai) Where is India?

Dekho: (they-kho) Look

Shabash: (shah-baash) Well done

Gulab jamuns: (goo-laab jaa-moons) Dough balls that are fried and soaked in sugar syrup, a popular dessert.

Kyon: (ki-yon') Why

Mein ghar kaise jaaungi? (mai ghur kay-say jaa-oon-gee) How will I go home?

Utho: (oo-thoe) Get up

Jaana hai: (jaa-nah hai) Have to go

Abhi nahin: (ub-bhee nuh-heen) Not now

The Indian food mentioned in the book is available at most Indian restaurants. For recipes please visit: www.orbolo.com.

Note from the Author

Many first and second generation immigrant children live between two worlds: the country their parents' migrated from and the country their family has chosen to live in. For many of these children contact with grandparents and other extended family members who live halfway across the world is limited, owing to their family's work and school schedules, travel restrictions and a variety of other reasons.

This story was inspired by my daughter's wish to ride a fast plane to spend the day with her grandparents, who live in India. At a very early age, Ishani understood that when she was eating breakfast in America, her grandparents were eating supper in India. The concept of day and night and the time differences across the countries is an intrinsic aspect of the two worlds that she experiences on an almost daily basis.

Language is an important vehicle for imparting awareness and understanding of one's cultural heritage and traditions to future generations. My purpose in writing this story using two languages is to highlight the bilingual communication patterns found in most immigrant families with origins in the Indian subcontinent. Using two or more languages in daily conversations is common in these families. Also, the bilingual nature of conversations between the grandparents and their grandchild in this book should be a familiar one to most readers with roots in southern Asia. Roman script was used for the second language to avoid the complexities associated with reading original scripts.

In addition to the language component, I have incorporated a knowledge component within the context of this story. My hope is that children will pick up the basic concept and look forward to exploring it in greater depth with their parents, teachers and friends.

I welcome all comments or suggestions from readers. Please feel free to send me email at cenakshi@gmail.com

Enakshi Choudhuri, Ph.D.
Minnesota, USA